Mindful Money Management
Aligning Wealth with Inner Peace

Table of Contents

Chapter 1. Introduction

Discover the profound synergy between financial health and personal peace in our Special Report: "Mindful Money Management: Aligning Wealth with Inner Peace". Dive into a world where personal finance does not have to be a source of stress but an avenue for tranquility, joy, and personal growth. Authored by renowned experts in the field, this engaging report uncovers the secrets to becoming financially secure while advancing on the path to inner peace, crucial in today's turbulent times. It's a fresh and uplifting exploration we believe everyone can benefit from. Once you've dipped your toes into this transformative approach, you'll want to plunge right in! Regardless of where you stand in your financial journey, learning to align your wealth with inner peace will not only enhance your financial acuity but will also elevate your overall quality of life. Give a gift to your future self by diving into mindful money management today.

Chapter 2. The Intersection of Wealth and Inner Peace

In the arena of personal finance, most people perceive wealth and inner peace as disparate concepts. People often compartmentalize financial wealth, associating it with stress, anxiety, and complexity, while they reserve inner peace for spiritual or emotional domains. This chapter aims to unite the two seemingly separate concepts, helping readers understand that true prosperity is an embodiment of financial health aligned with peace of mind.

2.1. The Equation of Wealth and Inner Peace

It is essential first to understand the correlation between wealth and inner peace in our lives. Often, one element is sacrificed in pursuit of the other, resulting in a sense of imbalance and dissatisfaction. Wealth, in this context, encompasses more than our financial status. It includes the abundance in different areas of our lives, such as time, relationships, health, and happiness. On the other hand, inner peace involves tranquility of mind, emotions, and spirit, often considered separate from our material lives.

When inner peace is absent, even the highest level of financial wealth can lead to dissatisfaction. On the contrary, a serene mind without wealth may bring about struggle and hardship. Striking the balance between the two by ensuring financial stability and inner tranquility is the focal point of this chapter.

2.2. Rethinking Wealth

Before we navigate the perception of wealth, it's important to understand that wealth is not an end in itself; instead, it serves as a tool to realize our dreams, maintain our lifestyles, and offer us comfort. However, wealth is not a guarantee of happiness or contentment. It merely provides the means to pursue those ends.

Shifting from a perspective of wealth as a source of happiness to one where wealth is just a tool can significantly lessen financial stress. This shift enables us to change our focus from purely material acquisition toward more holistic forms of wealth – like time spent with loved ones, physical health, hobbies, or personal growth. In essence, wealth is not the goal, but merely the means to realize our true priorities.

2.3. Cultivating Inner Peace Amidst Financial Endeavors

Inner peace forms the basis from which we can build a fulfilling life. Forming a positive relationship with money is an essential part of this process. We must first understand that our self-worth is inherent and is not determined by our financial worth. Money or material possessions are not measures of personal success or happiness. Detaching our identity from our financial status allows us to cultivate a sense of inner peace, irrespective of external circumstances.

Secondly, maintaining a positive mindset is crucial in this journey. Developing gratitude for what we already possess – whether material or immaterial – can profoundly alter our perception of wealth and happiness. Through gratefulness, we acknowledge the abundance already present in our lives, bringing fortitude in times of financial strain.

Moreover, adopting a mindset of sufficiency, where we consciously acknowledge that we have enough, can counteract the societal pressures of constant accumulation. This perspective promotes contentment and diminishes the fear of lack, connecting us to a state of peace and fulfilment.

2.4. The Synergy between Wealth and Inner Peace

Sustained financial health is intimately entwined with personal peace. How? It all comes down to the choices we make. When we make financial decisions from a state of peace, we are free from the distortions caused by fear or greed. Decisions guided by inner tranquility are likely to be focused on long-term financial health rather than short-term gains. This approach facilitates the building of wealth resilient to economic fluctuations, thus reducing the stress associated with money matters and contributing further to our overall peace of mind.

On the other hand, stable financial health can provide a secure base from which to explore and experience life, thereby enhancing our sense of inner peace. Financial stability can reduce anxiety and fear, creating space for personal growth, happiness, and contentment.

Balance here is key. Just as an overemphasis of financial considerations can threaten our peace of mind, excessive focus on tranquility at the cost of financial responsibilities can lead to financial strain and stress. It's the harmonious balance between wealth and inner peace that leads to a truly prosperous life.

2.5. Shaping a Future Aligned with Wealth and Inner Peace

The path towards aligning wealth with inner peace isn't necessarily easy, but it's rewarding. It starts with developing a clear understanding of our financial goals, aligning them with our personal values and priorities. This alignment serves to guide our financial decisions, ensuring that these choices reflect our true desires, leading to a sense of fulfilment and peace.

Moreover, honing financial skills such as budgeting, saving, investing, and tax planning not only ensures financial fitness but also reduces the stress and anxiety associated with money matters. Knowledge truly is power, and in the realm of personal finance, it is a vital tool for cultivating peace of mind and financial well-being.

In conclusion, the journey towards balancing financial wealth and inner peace is indeed a journey towards complete abundance, where financial prosperity and personal tranquility inform and reinforce each other. Though the path may seem daunting initially, the rewards of this holistic approach to personal finance are profound and enduring, leading to a life marked by wealth, happiness, and deep, abiding peace.

Chapter 3. Understanding Your Financial Stimuli and Responses

We are all affected by financial stimuli, but not everyone's response is the same. This variation is not just a matter of disposition or personality. Marrying finance and mindfulness can shine a light on the connection between our material world and inner thoughts, illuminating new pathways towards peace and prosperity.

3.1. Connection Between Finance and Emotion

The relationship between finance and emotion is hard to ignore. Every decision, small or large, involves an interplay of practical considerations and emotional factors. A raise in salary might heighten feelings of validation and recognition, while a monetary loss could trigger distress, anxiety, or insecurity. Understanding these responses, their roots, and implications is a critical stepping stone toward mindful money management.

However, these emotional responses are not innately negative. In fact, they can unlock powerful insights into our psychological blueprint and aid us in making better financial decisions going forward.

3.2. Identifying Financial Triggers

To leverage emotions to our advantage, we need to discern our financial triggers. A 'trigger' constitutes anything that prompts a certain behaviour or emotion. In the context of finance, this could be anything from a sizeable paycheck inflating self-worth or a surprise expense causing undue worry.

Staying aware of these triggers can help us make necessary adjustments and prevent impulsive decisions that could harm our financial health. This task involves a deep measure of self-awareness and mindfulness. Financial mindfulness, the practice of paying full attention to our financial activities and behaviours in a non-judgemental way, can substantially aid this process.

3.3. Crafting a Personal Money Narrative

Every individual has a unique money narrative, dictated by their past experiences, upbringing, and socio-economic background. Our financial behaviours, judgments, and inclinations are intricately tied to this narrative.

Reflecting on questions like "what money lessons did I learn growing up?" or "how has money influenced my relationships?" can reveal patterns that explain our financial stimuli and responses. We may find that much of our financial stress stems from this internal narrative, rather than external circumstances.

As we start rewriting our personal money narratives, we begin seeing money as a tool rather than a determinant of our worth or happiness. This transformation in perception can lead to improved financial decision-making and overall peace of mind.

3.4. Responding Mindfully to Financial Stimuli

Reacting to financial stimuli consciously involves creating that small space between stimulus and response where choice exists. It's about gaining control over our reactions rather than letting them control us.

To respond rather than react, we can employ mindfulness techniques such as deep breathing, stepping back, observing the thoughts and feelings, then choosing a response. These strategies not only help defuse the potent emotions around money but also promote empathy and compassion for others and ourselves, aiding in forgiveness for past financial faux pas.

3.5. Embracing Financial Education

Ignorance or misinformation about money matters can cause fear, uncertainty, and subsequent stress. One of the most effective ways to boost confidence and catalyze a positive emotional response toward finance is by seeking financial education.

We can pursue knowledge about budgeting, investing, retirement planning, debt management, and other financial facets. This wealth of knowledge will empower us to take ownership of our financial future, feed our curiosity, and still our financial anxieties.

3.6. Building a Money Presence Ritual

Instilling a ritual or practice around money can prove immensely beneficial. This might involve setting a specific time every week to review finances, track spending, or plan for upcoming expenses.

In doing so, we create a sense of routine and familiarity, rendering the task less daunting. Importantly, it keeps us present and engaged in managing our financial life.

3.7. Financial Future Visualization

Visualization exercises can be potent in shaping our financial behaviour and reactions. Imagine your life five or ten years down the line. What does financial success look like for you? How does it feel?

Creating a vivid mental image can provide motivation and direction. This practice opens the door to positive emotions around finance and provides a palpable goal to strive toward.

Our financial stimuli and responses are intricately tied to our beliefs, attitude, and emotions. With understanding, patience, and effort, we can consciously steer these emotions and reactions towards a healthier financial future and personal peace. The tools and techniques provided in this chapter serve as a compass guiding you towards mindful money management.

Chapter 4. Creating a Mindful Budget

The concept of a mindful budget emphasizes more than just mindful spending. It's about aligning your financial plan with your values, goals, and lifestyle. It focuses on being "present" in your financial decisions rather than being consumed by future anxieties or past regrets. By approaching budgeting with a mindful perspective, you're able to bring clarity and consciousness to your financial habits, decrease stress, make wise financial choices, and cultivate an overall sense of well-being. The following sections will discuss the steps involved in creating a mindful budget.

4.1. Understanding Your Current Financial Position

The initial step towards constructing a mindful budget is developing an understanding of your current financial position. This involves compiling data regarding your earnings, expenses, savings, and debts. Documenting this information gives you a clear picture of your financial health and helps pave the way for setting up a budget that aligns with your lifestyle and goals.

To do this, first list out your income sources along with their amounts. If your income fluctuates month by month, calculate an average. Following that, detail your monthly fixed costs like house rent, utilities, loan payments etc. Subsequently, note down your variable expenses such as groceries, dining, entertainment, etc. Lastly, summarize your savings, investments, and any outstanding debts.

These figures form the foundation of your budget. Keeping a close eye on them can preempt financial stress as you're better equipped to manage unexpected costs or changes in income.

4.2. Aligning Your Budget with Your Values and Goals

A key pillar in mindful budgeting is aligning your financial plan with your personal values and goals. Both short-term and long-term goals play a role in shaping your budget. Short-term goals could include saving for a vacation or creating an emergency fund, whereas long-term goals could involve saving for retirement or college education for your children.

Take some time to reflect on your values and how your budget could reflect those. For instance, if environmental sustainability is a core value, you may want to budget for products and services that align with this value. On the other hand, if personal growth and lifelong learning matter to you, your budget might include expenses for books, courses, and conferences.

By aligning your budget with your values and goals, you reinforce positive financial behaviors and habits. This alignment provides a sense of purpose to the otherwise tedious task of budget management.

4.3. Prioritizing Needs Over Wants

In mindful budgeting, there's a strong emphasis on differentiating between "needs" and "wants". This crucial distinction aids in managing scarce resources effectively.

Needs are essential expenses required for survival and could include housing, groceries, medical expenses, and transportation. Wants, on the other hand, are more of a luxury; they add an extra level of comfort or pleasure to your life but aren't necessary for survival.

Being able to identify and separate these categories in your budget has implications for your financial health. It sets the stage for mindful spending, where you're attuned to distinguishing essential expenditures from discretionary ones. This awareness can significantly help in keeping your spending in control, boosting savings, and reducing stress around finances.

4.4. Creating An Emergency Fund

An emergency fund provides a financial safety net in case of unexpected life events. These could be job loss, medical emergencies, or car repairs that could otherwise disrupt your day-to-day life and budget.

The ideal size of an emergency fund can vary based on your lifestyle, monthly costs, income, and dependents. A commonly recommended benchmark is to put away 3-6 months' worth of living expenses. This fund should ideally be kept in a liquid but low-risk account like a savings account.

By having an emergency fund, you have the peace of mind that should a financial disaster strike, you have the resources to remain resilient. This is not just financially prudent, but mentally and emotionally stabilizing too.

4.5. Adopting Best Practices for Mindful Budgeting

To create a truly mindful budget, you need to adopt certain best practices. These include regular check-ins on your budget, making necessary adjustments, practicing gratitude, and cultivating a mindset of abundance rather than scarcity.

Regular check-ins hold you accountable for your spending habits and help you align with your budgeting goals. Adjustments may be necessary as changes occur in income, expenses, or personal goals. Practicing gratitude for what you have reduces the urge to overspend while cultivating an abundance mindset helps you perceive budgeting as a tool for achieving your life's goals rather than as a restrictive activity.

Creating a mindful budget is a vital step toward financial health and personal peace. It supports decision-making, promotes financial freedom, and encourages stress-free management of personal finance. Its principles are not just applicable to individual expenditure, but also to societal and global economic health. Quite simply, it could be the cornerstone of personal wealth and inner peace management.

Chapter 5. The Art and Science of Conscious Spending

Spending is an integral part of our lives. We all have our share of expenses: from necessities like food, shelter, and healthcare, to wants like entertainment, gadgets, vacations, and more. However, the difference lies in how one spends - thoughtlessly or consciously? Most financial stress stems from the former. We'll explore how embracing the latter — conscious spending — can be a transformative journey toward financial health and personal peace.

5.1. The Concept of Conscious Spending

Conscious spending is about making informed, intentional decisions about where and how to allocate your resources. This concept transcends beyond merely budgeting or tracking expenses. It entails reflecting on our values, designing our spending to align with those values, and reaping the fruits of financial peace, satisfaction, and personal growth.

As a starting point, self-reflection is crucial. Ask yourself: "In the greater scheme of things, what matters most to me? What are my personal, professional, social, and spiritual goals?" These answers act as a compass, guiding you to assign your monetary resources effectively.

5.2. Linking Spending to Personal Values

After recognizing your values, the next step is linking expenditures to them. If a purchase doesn't align with these values, reconsider its necessity. Remember, every dollar spent on something unimportant is a dollar less for things that matter.

For instance, if you value your health, allocate resources for a nutritious diet, regular exercise, and medical care. If you want to support small businesses, think twice before purchasing from a multinational retail giant. When our spending reflects our beliefs, every expenditure feels satisfying, reducing stress and increasing peace of mind.

5.3. Calculations to Lead You Forward

Tracking expenses might seem tedious, but it's essential in understanding your spending habits. By noting down your expenses, either manually or with help of financial apps, you create a transparent picture of your finances. Categorize these into broad sections like necessities (rent, food), luxuries (eating out, gadgets), and savings (emergency fund, retirement). This clarity can be enlightening, highlighting superfluous costs and offering areas for a financial squeeze or expansion in alignment with your values.

Grasp the difference between expenditures that are fixed (mortgage, insurance), variable (groceries, utilities), and discretionary (entertainment, leisure travel). Note that even fixed costs may have room for modification; do we need a bigger house or a luxury car? Find potential flaws in current spending patterns and plan to corral them toward more conscious utilization.

5.4. Future-Oriented Conscious Spending

A crucial tenet of conscious spending is being future-oriented. Prioritize long-term wellbeing over short-term gratification. It doesn't mean you can't enjoy or indulge but emphasizes the importance of balance.

Consider how buying that expensive gadget will affect your financial health down the line. Does it prevent you from investing in yourself through education or experiences that could lead to substantial personal and financial growth? Weighing instant pleasure against long-term benefits promotes sound decision making and reinforces our commitment to aligning spending with personal values and goals.

5.5. Debt and Conscious Spending

Debt often incurs because of unconscious spending. The ease of 'swipe now, pay later' lures us into unnecessary expenditures, piling high interest-paying debts. Conscious spending advocates caution against falling into this trap.

If you find yourself burdened by debt, formulate a conscious plan for repayment. Prioritize high-interest debts, and create a reasonable timeframe for repayment. Avoid accumulating new debts unless they are crucial for your wellbeing or long-term personal and financial growth.

5.6. Conscious Spending for Peace and Prosperity

Adopting conscious spending doesn't imply compromising on joy or indulgences. It means spending in line with your values and goals without jeopardizing future financial security. When adopted, spending transforms from a source of stress into one of tranquility and personal growth.

As you practice conscious spending, you might observe a resonating peace manifesting within you because you know your monetary resources fuel your values and long-term goals. This financial acumen leads to growth and prosperity.

5.7. Implementing Conscious Spending Step by Step

Conscious spending can seem overwhelming when you begin, but dividing it into manageable steps can help:

1. Create a list of values and connect them to your financial goals.
2. Track expenses to understand and scrutinize your spending patterns.
3. Develop a financial plan that reflects these values, incorporating present needs, and future ambitions.
4. Regularly review and adjust this plan as per changing life circumstances and redefined goals.

Consistently following this process sets a strong foundation for achieving financial health and personal peace, cultivating a balanced and joyful lifestyle driven by mindful money management.

Embrace the art and science of conscious spending, and invite tranquility, joy, and substantial growth into your life. It's more than just about saving money – it's about spending wisely, which leads to financial freedom and inner peace. Happy conscious spending!

Chapter 6. Avoiding Financial Anxiety: Practices and Habits

Financial anxiety is a common problem that is rarely examined separately from the broader issue of financial health. However, it entails much more than just numbers on a balance sheet. It's about the emotional turmoil caused by money troubles: the stress, the worry, the fear, the paralyzing inaction and resistance to growth. Left unchecked, these feelings can rob you of a sense of peace and tranquility, interfering with not only your financial wellness but also your mental and emotional wellbeing.

6.1. Identifying Financial Anxiety

Firstly, recognize that financial anxiety is not an anomaly that affects a handful of individuals but a widespread issue. How can you identify if you're dealing with financial anxiety? Not knowing whether your money will stretch enough to pay your monthly bills, worrying about losing everything due to unexpected circumstances, or constantly fearing the downfall of your financial security are all signs of financial anxiety.

Understanding that this is a problem and accepting your situation is the first essential approach towards a solution. Once identified, it's time to respond. Are you ready to move from emotional turmoil to a mindful financial practice that brings calm and peacefulness? It's not an overnight transition but a continual practice that you can refine over time.

6.2. The Buffer of Emergency Savings

Remember the adage, "save for a rainy day"? It's not just an old wives' tale but a critical financial measure. An emergency savings fund acts as a buffer against unexpected events such as losing your job, unforeseen medical expenses, or urgent car repairs.

How much should you have stashed away? A common recommendation is a sum equivalent to six months of your living expenses. Build your fund steadily, even if it means setting aside a small portion of your income each month. Having that safety net can ease your mind substantially, giving you a sense of security and reducing the stress associated with financial uncertainly.

6.3. The Peace of Being Insured

Insurance is another effective way to cope with financial worries. Health insurance, car insurance, life insurance, home insurance, and renters' insurance all serve to safeguard your financial stability. These policies protect against big, unexpected expenses.

However, insurance policies are not built equally. It's important to understand the terms, conditions, and limits of each policy you own. Review your policies regularly to make sure they meet your changing needs and circumstances.

6.4. The Tranquility of a Budget

Imagine trying to reach a destination without knowing the path. This is precisely what happens when you juggle your finances without a budget.

Creating and following a budget provides a roadmap towards

financial peace. It enables you to consciously decide how to spend and save, making sure your money is working for you. Remember, a budget isn't about restricting what you spend but helping you spend without guilt or worry. When executed effectively, budgeting can bolster your savings, decrease your debt, and alleviate your financial anxiety.

6.5. The Courage to Seek Professional Help

Sometimes, it might seem like no matter what steps you take, you're stuck in your cycle of financial stress. Know that it's okay to seek help. A personal finance advisor can assist with effective strategies for managing your wealth. They can help you understand areas of improvement, set realistic goals, and track your progress.

Similarly, if your financial stressors are causing persistent distress, a mental health professional can equip you with strategies to cope. Just as you would seek medical attention for a broken leg, mental and emotional health should be handled with the same urgency and care.

6.6. The Freedom of Living Within Your Means

Living within your means is an age-old wisdom that has stood the test of time. This doesn't imply a life of frugality but rather understanding the boundaries of your financial capabilities. When you live within or below your means, you minimize the risk of debt, promoting a sense of financial security and independence.

6.7. Final Reflection

Addressing your financial anxiety and cultivating habits that foster financial peace is not a one-size-fits-all process. The key is to know that your financial health is not separate from your personal peace. Navigate your money matters with mindfulness, patience, and persistent action, and enjoy the journey towards aligning your wealth with inner peace.

Remember, the goals are long-term tranquility and financial security, not fleeting moments of financial satisfaction built on shaky grounds.

Chapter 7. Sustainable Investing as a Path to Peace

Investing often comes with the perception of a frantic, fast-paced environment that thrives on aggressive strategies and a focus on conventional returns. However, there's an alternative path you can follow. A course where investing can become a journey towards social consciousness, ecological balance, and indeed, personal peace. This journey is 'Sustainable Investing,' and it's not merely a trendy buzzword. It's a way of financial decision-making that aligns with your personal values, contributing to your sense of inner peace and overall wellbeing.

7.1. Sustainable Investing: An Overview

Sustainable investing is about incorporating environmental, social, and governance (ESG) factors into investment decisions for better-managed companies and improved societal outcomes. It's a way of acknowledging that the decisions we make with our money can have profound impacts on our world.

Sustainable investing enables us to use our financial resources to aid companies and industries that mirror our values—whether it's about maintaining ecological balance, endorsing social justice, or practicing sound governance. By doing so, our investments become aligned, not just with our financial aspirations, but also our moral, ethical, and social beliefs. This alignment creates an inherent sense of tranquility and fulfillment, a satisfying knowledge that our money is working for us and the larger good.

7.2. Aligning Investments with Your Values

Utilizing your investments as a tool to create a more sustainable and accountable business environment fosters a deeper connection with the world around you. It's not merely about the financial return; it becomes about the impact your money can make.

When your investments reflect your values, you're no longer isolated from the process. You become an active participant, with the knowledge that your money is working to foster change, not just in your financial health but also the health of society and the environment.

Many investors find that this connection reduces anxiety and stress associated with investing. It transforms the practice from being a mere number game to creating a meaningful impact that supports a shared, sustainable future.

7.3. Choosing the Right Sustainable Investment

The first step towards sustainable investing is choosing the right place to invest. Sustainability-conscious investors often look at two primary areas: ESG scores and impact investing.

ESG score measurement is a tool used by investors to screen companies based on their environmental, social, and governance performances. Companies with high ESG scores are deemed to be more responsible towards these issues and are typically preferred by sustainable investors.

Impact investing, on the other hand, directly focuses on companies aiming to bring about positive change in social or environmental sectors. Here, the investment considerations are not merely about financial returns; they focus on a more holistic and sustainable impact.

Choosing the right investment needs careful consideration of your financial goals, risk tolerance, and most importantly, your social and environmental convictions.

7.4. Role of Financial Advisor

Working with a financial advisor who understands and respects sustainable investing can be invaluable on this journey. They can help identify investment opportunities that are in line with both your financial goals and your personal values.

A well-informed advisor will guide you through the complexities of ESG scoring, help you understand impact investing better, and assist you in making choices that enrich your financial health and contribute towards social and environmental wellness.

7.5. The Long-Term Payoff

Sustainable investing is not only about making a positive impact. Studies suggest that companies with higher ESG scores often demonstrate better operational performance and are less risky. Moreover, during market downturns, sustainable investments tend to be more resilient.

The core idea of sustainable investing aligns with the principle of inner peace – it's a long-term commitment. Investors who aim for quick gains may find it hard to align with this principle. But for those who view their financial health as a lifelong journey, sustainable investing can bring balance and satisfaction.

7.6. Conclusion: Sustainable Investing for Inner Peace

The essence of sustainable investing lies in its ability to merge financial goals with personal values, creating an investment strategy that contributes to personal peace—a sense of fulfillment and tranquility that stems from knowing your finances serve a purpose beyond mere growth.

Sustainable investing may not provide the adrenaline rush that short-term, aggressive strategies might offer. However, it offers something profoundly more satisfying - the knowledge that your money is working for a cause, contributing to a more sustainable and equitable world. Through sustainable investing, you don't just create financial security - you contribute to a world you'd be proud to leave behind for future generations.

Remember, investing need not be a frantic race to financial security. It can be a conscious journey toward a sustainable future and personal peace when approached with mindfulness. Let your money reflect who you are and the difference you wish to see in the world. Turn their synergy into a source of tranquility, joy, and personal growth. With sustainable investing, you're not just managing your money mindfully; you're paving a path to inner peace.

Chapter 8. Empowerment Through Financial Literacy

Financial literacy is often the cornerstone to financial freedom. Only by understanding the intricacies of finance can one truly harness the power to leverage their money for long-term growth and prosperity. Acquiring skills such as budgeting, money management, understanding investments, and investigating income generation possibilities are all critical steps in cultivating financial literacy.

8.1. Understanding Financial Literacy

To embark on the journey of financial literacy, it's important to establish clear definitions. At its core, financial literacy describes the understanding of various financial principles and the mastery of skills necessary to make informed decisions about all financial aspects of one's life. It encompasses a wide range of areas, from everyday budgeting and personal savings, to complex investment choices, and understanding economic indicators impacting personal finance.

Financial literacy enables an individual to plan for their future, save for emergencies, and become self-sufficient. Without financial literacy, individuals often find themselves in precarious situations, such as taking on bad debts, being unable to save, or failing to plan for retirement.

8.2. The Importance of Budgeting

Beginning with everyday budgeting, one of the most foundational aspects of financial literacy, helps individuals understand where their money comes from and where it goes. Budgeting allows one to track income, outline expenses, and ensure that funds are allocated to important areas such as savings, investments, and debt repayments. A good budget not only establishes a plan for current spending but also lays down a roadmap for future financial decisions.

The first step toward building a budget is tracking income and expenses. Understand your regular income sources - be it salary, investments, freelance work, etc. Simultaneously, list all your regular expenses, from the smallest expenditures, like a cup of coffee or a monthly app subscription, to larger ones like rent/mortgage payments or tuition.

After identifying income and expenses, organize these figures into categories. Common income categories include salaries/wages, investment income, or business income. Expenditure categories could be general living expenses, discretionary spendings like entertainment or eating out, and financial goals like paying off debt faster, saving for a holiday, or investing for retirement.

8.3. Achieving Savings Goals

Savings are like a lifeboat in the ocean of uncertain economic conditions. No matter how much income one earns, if they aren't saving, they're putting their financial health at risk. Financial literacy empowers individuals to understand the importance of savings and how to effectively achieve their savings goals.

One of the most important principles of saving is "paying yourself first." This means, before spending money on any expenses, allocate a portion of your income to your savings. The amount of savings would be primarily dictated by your financial goals. These goals could be general (like having a 3-6 months emergency fund), medium-term (like saving for a down payment for a house), or long-term (like accumulating a retirement corpus).

8.4. Building a Strong Investment Portfolio

While saving is an integral part of financial health, merely saving money and leaving it idle in a bank account is not enough. To grow your wealth and achieve long-term financial stability, investing is key. Financial literacy helps individuals understand the risks and rewards associated with various types of investments and create an investment portfolio that matches their risk tolerance and financial goals.

Financially literate individuals are better equipped to navigate the complex world of investments. They're more likely to understand the difference between stocks, bonds, mutual funds, and other forms of investments.

They also understand the concept of risk and reward and diversification. Understanding that higher rewards often come with higher risks and spreading investments across different assets class, regions, or sectors, can reduce risk and stabilize returns.

8.5. Navigating the Debt Landscape

Another critical area of focus in the path to financial literacy is understanding debt. When leveraged wisely, debt can be a powerful tool in achieving financial goals. However, without the proper knowledge to navigate the debt landscape, it can turn into a burdensome entity that causes unnecessary stress and financial hardship.

This part of financial literacy involves understanding interest rates and the impact of different loan terms, recognizing the dangers of bad debts and how to avoid them, and knowing about managing existing debts. Financial literacy empowers individuals with the strategies needed to manage their debts wisely.

In conclusion, the path to achieving financial literacy is a journey that demands time, patience, and dedication. As we dive deeper into each area, the puzzle pieces of this complex field fall into place, leading to autonomous, confident decision-making related to all aspects of personal finance. Achieving a high level of financial literacy paves the way for empowerment, enabling individuals to take control of their financial destinies while cultivating a sense of peace, tranquility, and security within their lives, thereby aligning wealth with inner peace.

Chapter 9. Debt Management: The Path to Financial Freedom

Debt, a word that comes laden with heavy negative connotations for many. Burdened with anxieties and fears, individuals often grapple with the intricate maze of liabilities. However, debt doesn't necessarily signal disaster, nor does it need to eclipse your peace. Efficient Debt Management can pave the way to financial freedom while discerning the techniques to utilize it as a valuable tool for your financial repertoire. The underlying rule is simple - proper organization, understanding, and management, followed by sensible planning and consistency. Now, let's delve deeper into this pragmatic approach.

9.1. The Nature of Debt: Understanding its Necessity

Comprehending the nature of debt is an initial step. Commonly, debt is perceived as negative. Regrettably, this negative connotation is often associated with poor financial decisions leading to vicious cycles of indebtedness. However, borrowing money is not inherently a bad idea; it only becomes destructive when mishandled.

Debt can be a brilliant tool when used wisely. It can provide the leverage necessary to rise above circumstances, may it be buying our first home, getting a university education, or starting a new business. Responsibly managed, debt can be instrumental in achieving significant milestones and riding the tide towards financial freedom. Recognizing this facet of debt can be a transformative shift in your relationship with money, facilitating peaceful coexistence.

9.2. Debt Demystified: Types and Impacts

Understanding the type and impact of different debts on our financial health is crucial. Not all debts are created equal, and distinguishing between 'good' and 'bad' debt can help you manage your debts more effectively.

- 'Good' Debt: This is a type of debt that can benefit your financial future over the long term. It's an investment that will grow in value or generate long-term income. An example could be a home mortgage or student loans.

- 'Bad' Debt: This is incurred when you borrow to purchase depreciating assets or consumable items. Credit card debts incurred due to lifestyle expenses fall under this category.

The key is to leverage good debt and reduce bad debt to remain in the healthy financial spectrum.

9.3. The Debt Snowball and Avalanche: Prioritizing Your Debts

There are several techniques to prioritize and pay off your debts effectively. Two of the most common and equally effective methods are – The Debt Snowball and The Debt Avalanche.

In the 'Debt Snowball' method, you start by focusing on the smallest debt first, regardless of the interest rate. This method centers on the psychological win of paying off a debt in full, which builds momentum and motivation to tackle bigger debts.

In contrast, the 'Debt Avalanche' method advocates paying off the debt with the highest interest rate first. This may save you more in the long run, yet it requires a strong resolve as it may take longer to see progress.

Both methods have their merits, and the choice depends on your personal preference and discipline.

9.4. Creating a Debt Management Plan

A Debt Management Plan (DMP) is a structured strategy that helps you deal with outstanding debts. This involves setting up a budget, prioritizing debts, and determining a set amount to pay off every month. Here's a basic step-by-step guide:

1. List all your debts, including the debt amounts, interest rates, and minimum monthly payments.

2. Prioritize your debts using either the Snowball or Avalanche method.

3. Allocate a minimum payment for each debt.

4. Create a realistic budget, outlining your income and expenses.

5. Dedicate a part of your income to repay debts.

6. Review on a monthly basis and adjust as required.

A Debt Management Plan, coupled with discipline and determination, can be a vital tool for achieving a debt-free life.

9.5. Negotiating with Creditors

It can be daunting to approach your creditors, but communication is key. Most lenders are open to the idea of setting up a repayment plan that works for both parties. They would rather see partial repayment over no repayment. Honest and timely communication can help save your credit score, reduce your stress, and also avoid legal procedures.

As you start to manage your debts efficiently, you'll start noticing a shift in your financial and personal wellbeing. By treating debt not as an enemy, but as an aspect to gain control over, you carve the path towards financial freedom. Proper debt management can significantly influence your journey towards achieving inner peace. After all, financial peace is not just about wealth accumulation, it's being able to sleep at night knowing that your bills are paid, your future is secured, and your life is well within your control. As with any personal development journey, remember that debt management is a process, and it's perfectly normal to experience stumbles. The important aspect is to pick yourself up and keep going, and gradually, you'll discover the peace and financial freedom you were seeking.

Chapter 10. Cultivating Prosperity: Aligning Your Financial Goals with Your Values

Embracing prosperity requires more than acquiring digits in your bank account. It's about welcoming abundance in all aspects of life, meticulously sowed and nurtured by the seeds of wise decisions and actions. And at the core of such decisions and actions lie your values—your deep-rooted beliefs, ideals, principles. Aligning your financial decisions with your values paves the way for prosperity weaved with the fabric of personal satisfaction, contentment, and feeling of success. This understanding is the cornerstone of thriving both financially and emotionally.

10.1. The Power of Personal Values

Personal values are the compass that guides your decisions and actions in life. They are the foundation upon which your life's principles, ideals, and potential achievements are built. Every decision you make, particularly financial ones, must be strongly rooted in your values. Only then can you start cultivating prosperity that goes beyond the material definition.

It's crucial to remember that your values might differ significantly from those of the people around you. Be it simplicity, freedom, security, philanthropy, or success, what matters is how well your financial decisions harmonize with your core values. This harmony promotes not just wealth accumulation but a feeling of satisfaction and accomplishment.

10.2. Understanding Your Values

Before aligning your finances with your values, you must understand what those values are. Identifying your values isn't about choosing a few desirable traits from a list; it involves deep introspection to know what truly drives you, fills you with passion, and represents your 'self'.

There are various ways of identifying personal values. You can reflect on moments in your life when you felt the happiest, proudest, or fulfilled. Identify what was crucial to those moments—these are likely linked to your values. Likewise, evaluating challenging moments in life can reveal values that you find important but weren't honored then.

10.3. Aligning Your Financial Goals With Your Values

Once you've nailed down your values, you can begin aligning your financial goals accordingly.

For instance, if one of your core values is family and community, tailored financial goals could be securing a comfortable life for your family, investing in your children's education, or supporting community development initiatives. Alternatively, if your primary value is freedom, your goals might be related to achieving financial independence, travel, or starting your own business.

The alignment of your financial goals with your values transforms the pursuit of wealth into a fulfilling journey. It no longer becomes about just accumulating more but about celebrating the values that shape who you are.

10.4. Financial Decisions: A Reflection of Your Values

Financial decisions are like a mirror reflecting your values. From savings and investments to spending and donation choices—they should all reflect what you cherish most in life. Authentic alignment will prevent any disconnect between what you believe in and what your financial decisions entail.

Suppose you value environmental sustainability. In that case, you might prefer investing in green businesses that prioritize environmental responsibility or purchase products from companies that support sustainable practices.

Remember, each financial decision crafted around your values propels you closer to personal and financial tranquility.

10.5. Mindful Spending & Investing

Mindful spending involves making purchasing decisions that echo your personal values. It's about recognizing needs over wants and prioritizing expenditures that appreciate in value, contribute to your goals, or enhance your well-being.

On the other hand, mindful investing is about supporting businesses and causes that resonate with your values. Whether it's investing in a company based on its social responsibility, business ethics, or the products and services it offers; making investment decisions based on values can bring both financial return and personal satisfaction.

Recognize that aligning your financial decisions involves occasional sacrifices. Extravagance might need to be curbed, instant gratification might need to be tamed, and patience should become your friend. These sacrifices are not about restraining but about empowering yourself with conscious choices that augment your financial and personal growth.

10.6. Roadmap to Prosperity

Creating a roadmap from your current financial state to your envisioned future based on your values can be highly rewarding. Having a clear path to follow can help you stay on track when you're tempted to stray due to the allure of a quick win or a perceived shortcut to wealth.

The roadmap will look different for everyone, but it generally includes an emergency fund, getting out of or managing debt, setting both short-term and long-term goals, saving, investing, philanthropy, and leaving a legacy.

This roadmap operates as your tailored guidebook steering your financial decisions and actions, helping you remain steadfast amidst the ever-changing financial landscapes.

Cultivating prosperity by aligning your financial goals with your values is an enlightening endeavor. This alignment creates a harmonious relationship between your finances and personal peace, allowing you to freely steer towards prosperous shores. It yields not only financial rewards but also inner tranquility and profound joy that come from living in tune with personal values. You not only get to build your wealth, but you get to define what wealth means to you—and that is true prosperity

Chapter 11. The Mindful Money Recap: Achieving Wealth and Inner Peace

Financial stability and personal peace often seem like two entirely different, even conflicting, aspects of life. Yet, they hold the potential to work hand in hand in producing not just a successful individual, but a holistic one. Leaning into the synergy between them could shape a path that not only leads to financial security but also propels one towards tranquility, joy, and personal growth.

11.1. Understanding Wealth and Inner Peace

Wealth is often equated to possessing ample sums of money or property, but in the grander scheme of things, its definition extends far beyond the material. Wealth embodies peace of mind, freedom of choice, and the ability to enjoy life's experiences. The concept closely ties with our inner peace—an internal state of calmness, contentment, and joy, regardless of external circumstances.

It is notable that wealth and inner peace are mutual enablers. The absence of financial worries paves the way for peace, while inner tranquility provides the clarity necessary for effective money management. Thus, understanding how both these concepts intertwine crucially sets the primary foundation for mindful money management.

11.2. The Principles of Financial Health

Financial health echoes your ability to meet financial obligations, cushion yourself from unforeseen circumstances, and plan for the future. Key to achieving this is understanding fundamental financial principles.

1. **Budgeting:** A budget offers a clear picture of your income, expenses, and potential savings. It helps recognize areas of extravagant expenditures and opportunities to save.

2. **Saving:** An integral component of financial security, it provides a financial buffer during unexpected financial hardships (medical bills, job loss, etc.) and allows long-term financial planning (retirement, starting a business, etc.).

3. **Investing:** An acceleration strategy for wealth accumulation, investments in stocks, bonds, or mutual funds can often help money to grow over time.

4. **Insurance:** A strategic risk management step, insurances safeguard you against potentials risks and financial losses.

5. **Debt Management:** Handling debts effectively by either starting to pay off the ones with the highest interest rates first or by consolidating multiple debts streamlines finances.

However, mere knowledge of these principles is not enough until they are coherently and consistently applied.

11.3. Achieving Financial Health

Attaining financial health, similar to reaching a state of physical health, demands time, patience, and consistent effort. It begins with creating comprehensive financial plans that align with your life goals and personal values. Additionally, educating oneself about personal finance basics, adopting healthy money habits, creating achievable financial goals, and seeking professional advice when appropriate, are all important steps in this process.

You should nurture a habit of regular financial checkups—assessments that can help ensure your relationship with money remains healthy and beneficial. Meanwhile, always be prepared to adjust and adapt your financial plans with changing circumstances and opportunities.

11.4. Cultivating Inner Peace

Inner peace, often elusive amidst hectic modern life, can elude our grasp unless we deliberately seek it. The pursuit of inner peace involves intentional practices to calm our minds, manage stress, and cultivate mindfulness.

1. **Mindfulness:** Regularly practicing mindfulness contributes to inner peace by helping us stay in the present moment instead of worrying about the past or future.

2. **Meditation:** Regular meditation fosters a sense of calm and balance, reducing stress, increasing relaxation, and enhancing overall well-being.

3. **Gratitude:** Cultivating an attitude of gratitude helps shift focus away from negative experiences, promoting happiness, reducing stress, and encouraging an overall peaceful demeanor.

4. **Emotional Intelligence:** Being aware and managing your emotions skillfully helps maintain inner equilibrium, even during challenging times.

11.5. Aligning Wealth with Inner Peace: The Mindful Money Approach

Mindful Money Management is an integrative approach that blends financial literacy with mindfulness practices, leveraging the synergy between financial health and inner peace.

Seeking balance between 'Making Money' and 'Making Peace' and aligning financial behaviors with personal values and goals becomes paramount in this process. Through making conscientious spending and saving decisions, one may foster both financial sustainability and personal well-being.

A significant aspect is acknowledging money emotions—the often unspoken feelings and attitudes about money that subtly influence financial decisions—and understanding their root cause. By paying attention to these emotions and their effects on financial behaviors, you can start to untangle unhealthy money habits and replace them with more beneficial ones.

11.6. Practical Mindful Money Techniques

1. **Money Mantras:** Use positive affirmations as money mantras to influence subconscious money narratives. Repeat phrases like "Money is a tool for my wellbeing" or "I create healthy money habits" regularly.

2. **Money Journaling:** Journal your money emotions, spending decisions, and financial goals. This reflection helps to recognize patterns, shifts your mindset, and promotes financial mindfulness.

3. **Mindful Spending Practices:** Ask yourself if a purchase aligns with your values and needs. This mindful examination can significantly decrease impulsive buying and improve money management.

4. **Consistent Financial Education:** Regular learning nurtures informed financial decisions. Devote time to understanding and updating about financial trends, investing strategies, and personal finance management.

In summary, this mindful money approach invites you to reflect, reassess, and reinvent your relationship with money by taking calculated, conscientious financial decisions. The result: A transformed financial journey characterized by wealth enhancement and personal growth aligned with the pursuit of inner peace.

Adopting Mindful Money Management is not a one-step miracle, but a consistent practice and lifelong learning process. However, the journey's rewards—a robust financial footing and profound inner tranquility—make it a pursuit worth undertaking. In the grand scheme of life's pursuit, aligning wealth and inner peace is a keynote harmony that could orchestrate the symphony of personal success, peace, abundance, and life satisfaction.

www.ingramcontent.com/pod-product-compliance
Lightning Source LLC
Chambersburg PA
CBHW062304290526
45794CB00006B/2694

* 9 7 9 8 8 5 8 3 1 8 6 0 6 *